Houseplant Lover
Coloring Book

by Beehive 95 Designs

© 2021 Jamie Kazmercyk

beehive95designs@gmail.com
www.beehive95designs.com
Illustrations by Jamie Kazmercyk

ISBN: 9798654008015
Imprint: Independently
published

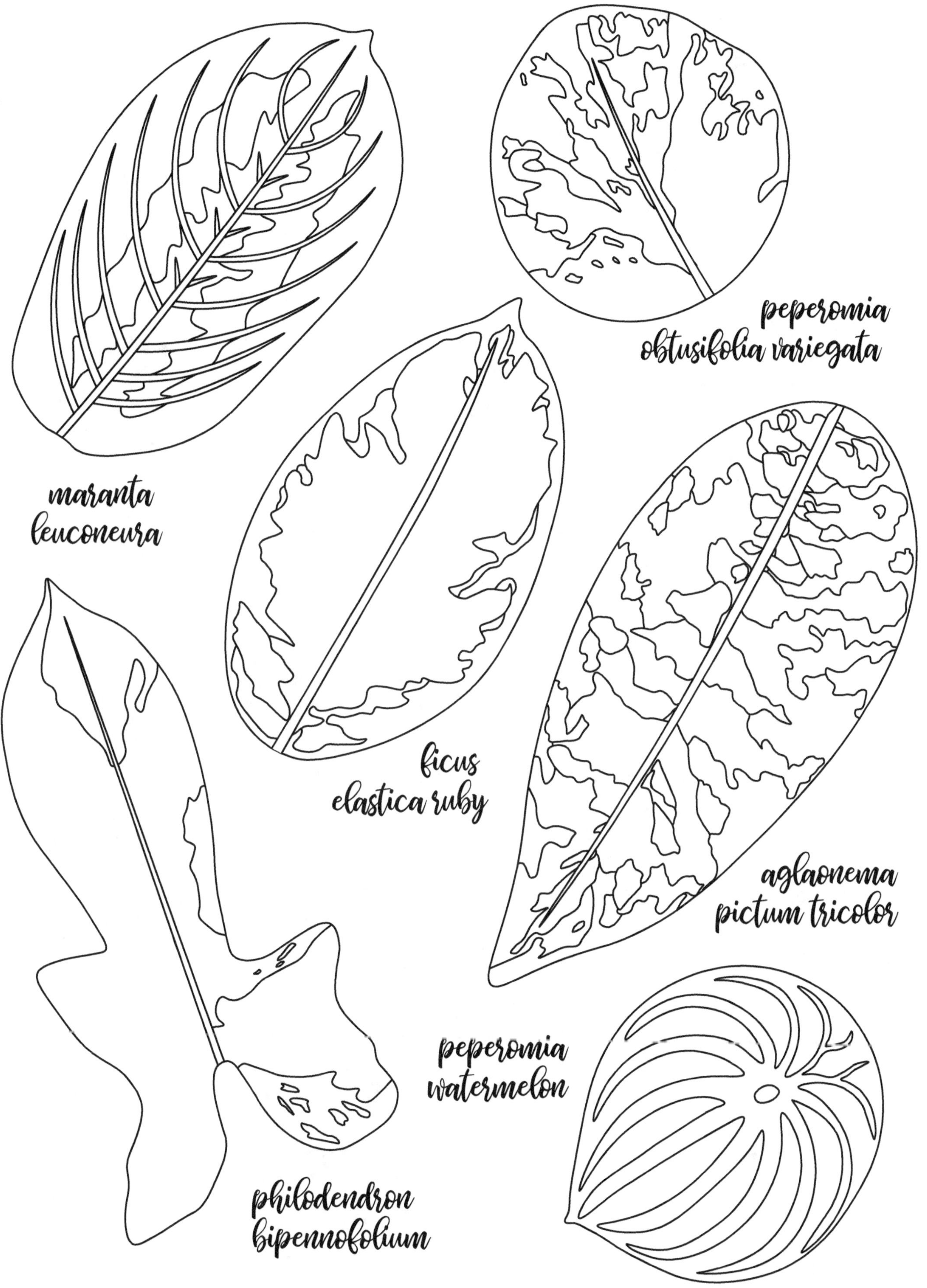

maranta
leuconeura

peperomia
obtusifolia variegata

ficus
elastica ruby

aglaonema
pictum tricolor

peperomia
watermelon

philodendron
bipennofolium

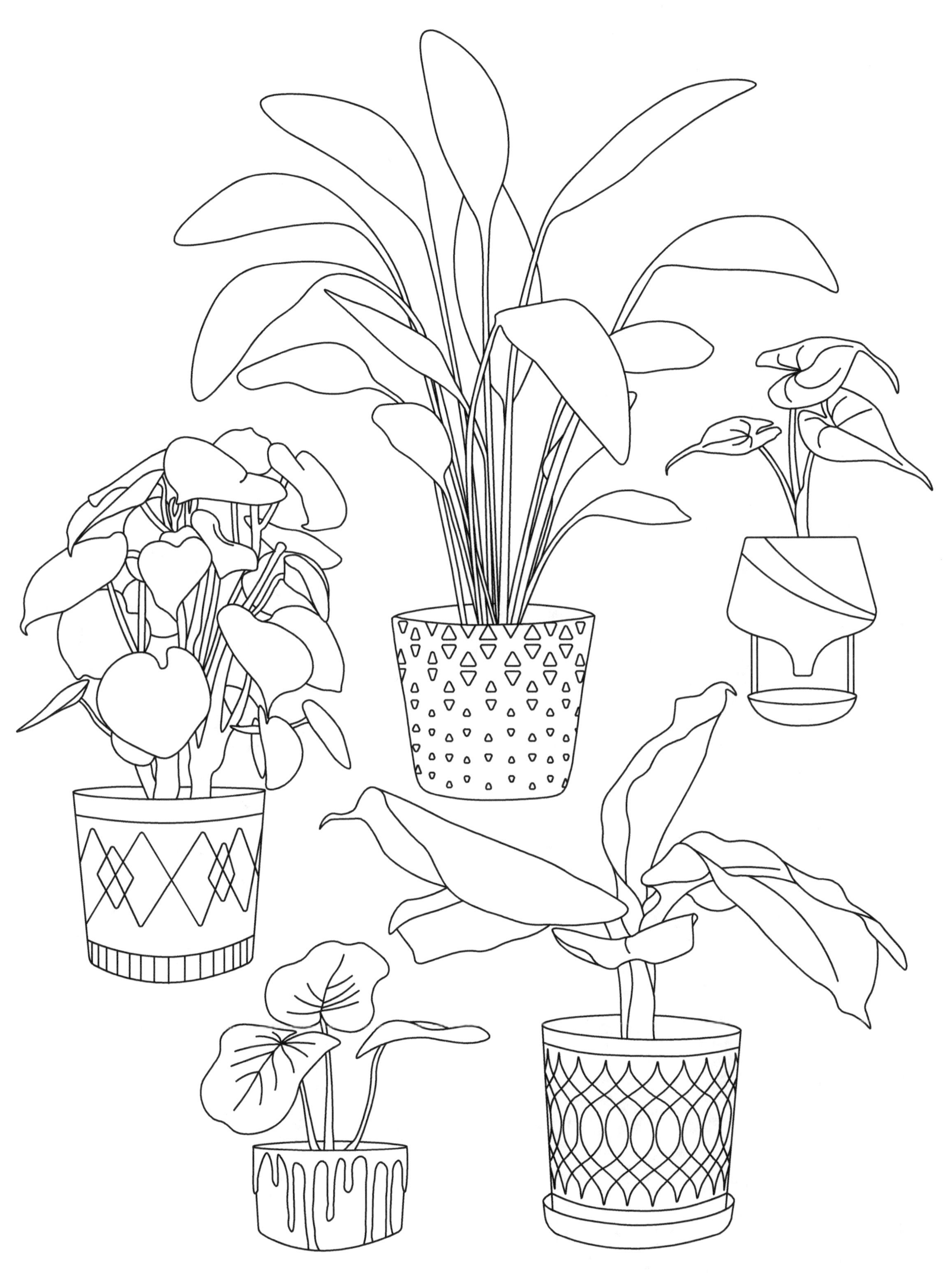

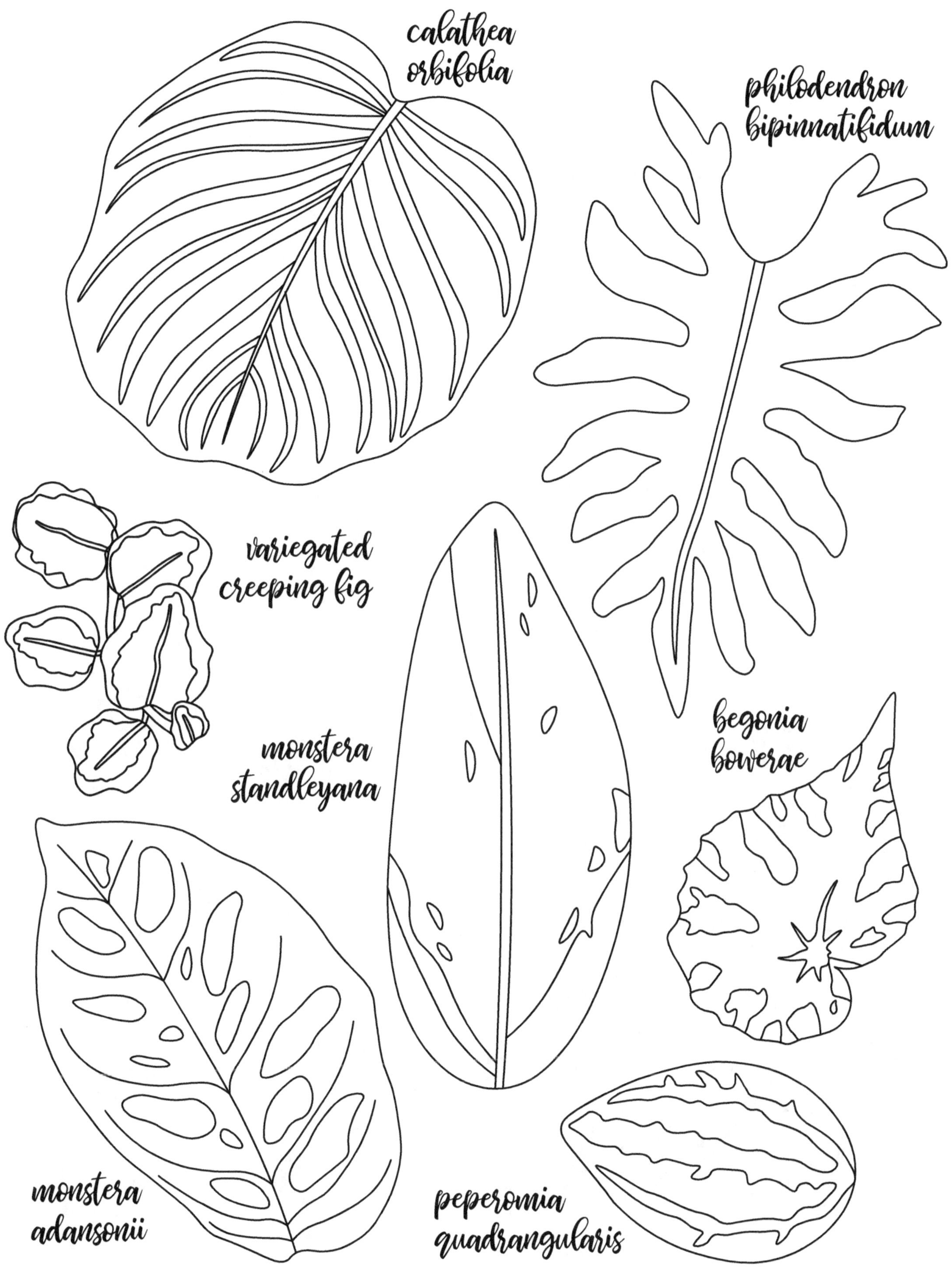

calathea
orbifolia
philodendron
bipinnatifidum
variegated
creeping fig
begonia
bowerae
monstera
standleyana
monstera
adansonii
peperomia
quadrangularis

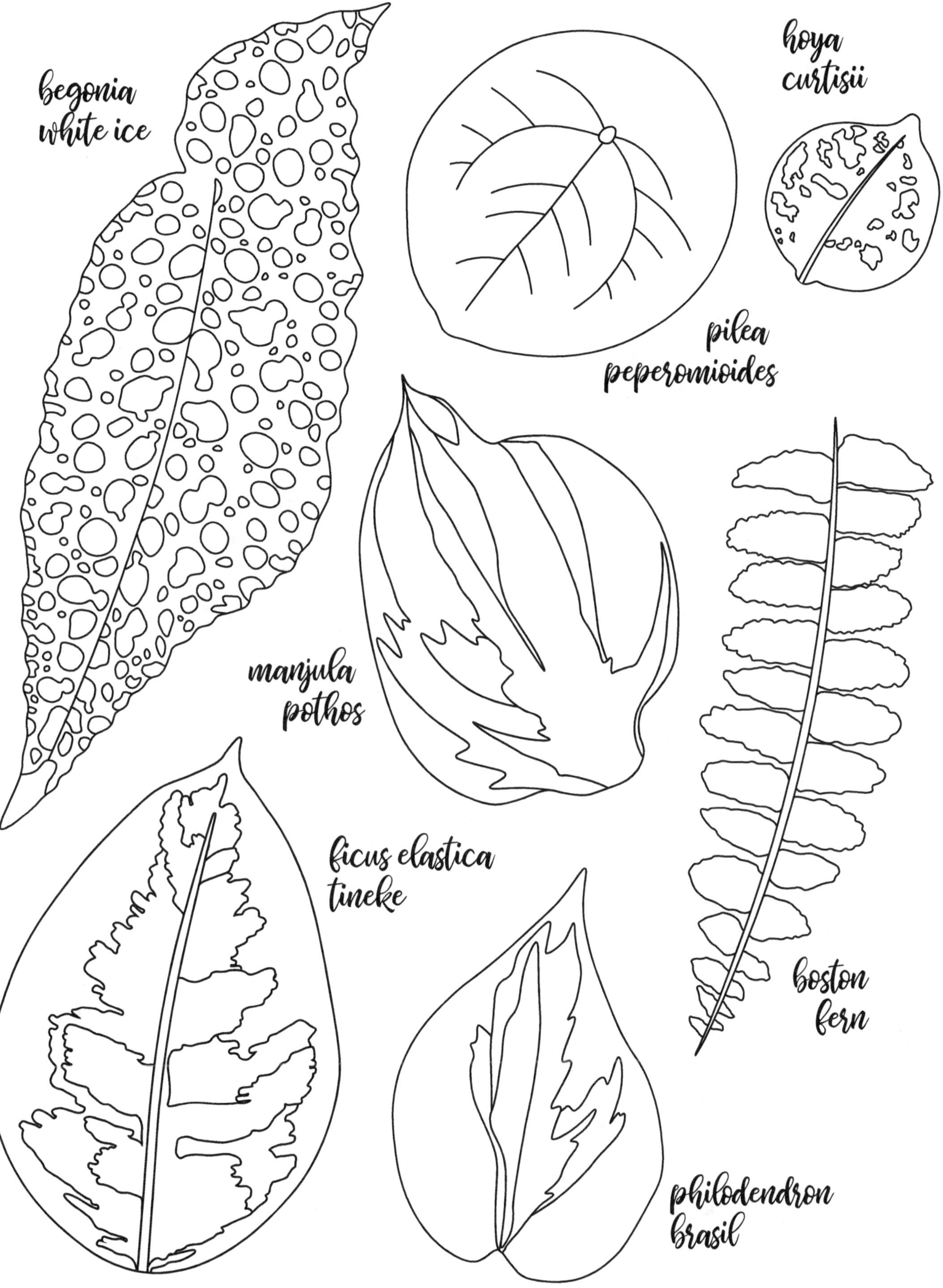

begonia
white ice
hoya
curtisii
pilea
peperomioides
manjula
pothos
ficus elastica
tineke
boston
fern
philodendron
brasil

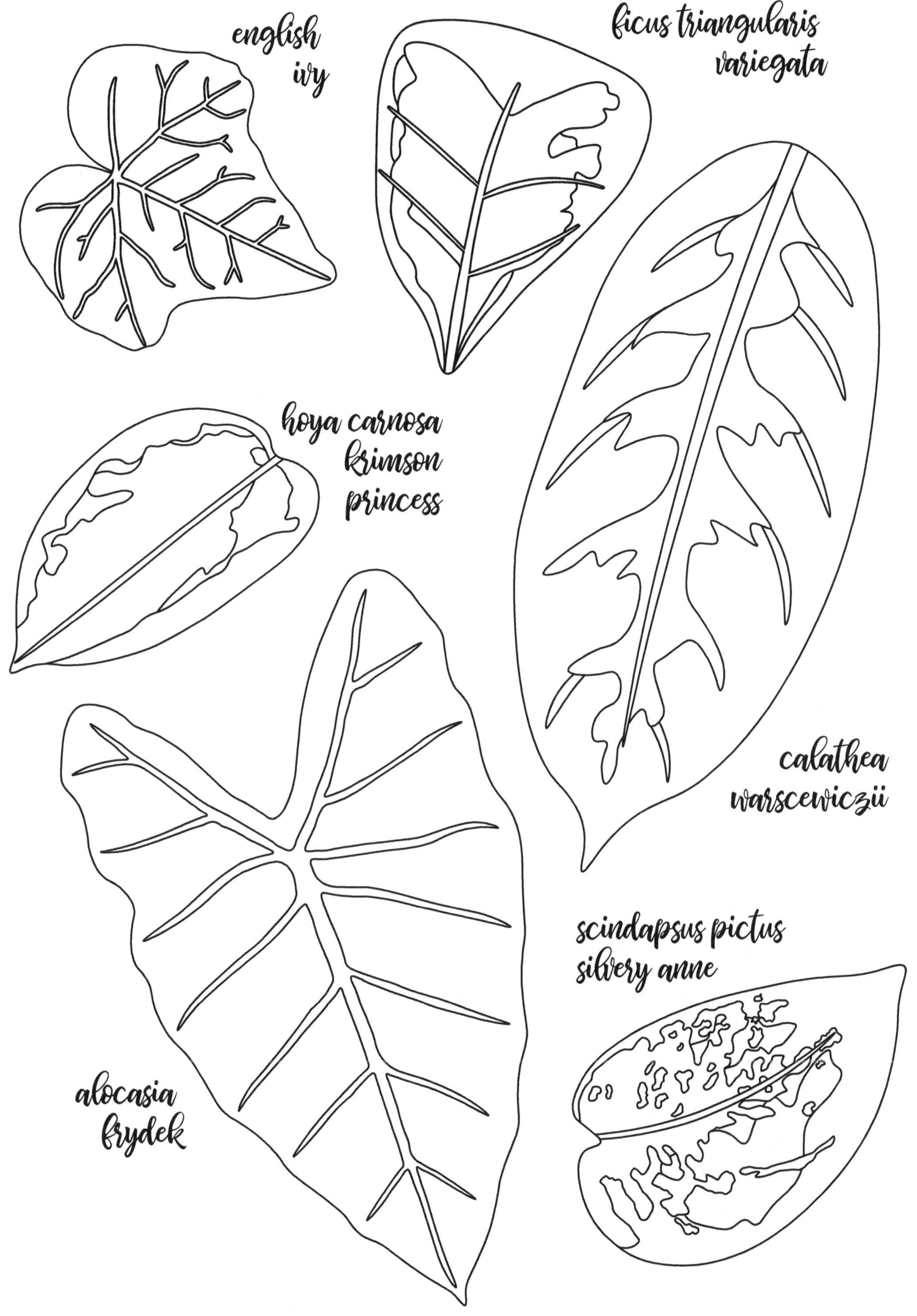
english
ivy
ficus triangularis
variegata
hoya carnosa
krimson
princess
calathea
warscewiczii
scindapsus pictus
silvery anne
alocasia
frydek

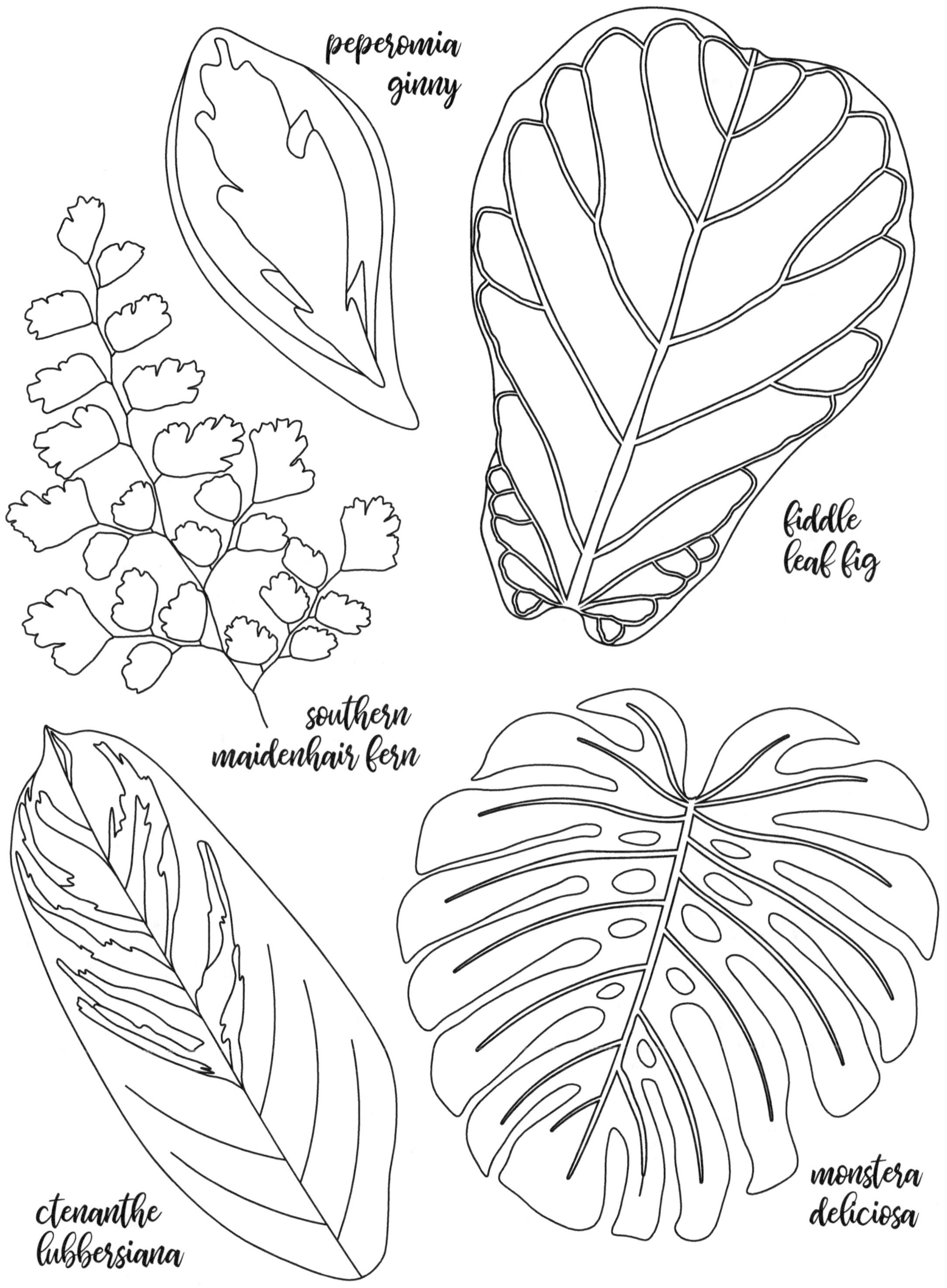

peperomia
ginny
fiddle
leaf fig
southern
maidenhair fern
ctenanthe
lubbersiana
monstera
deliciosa

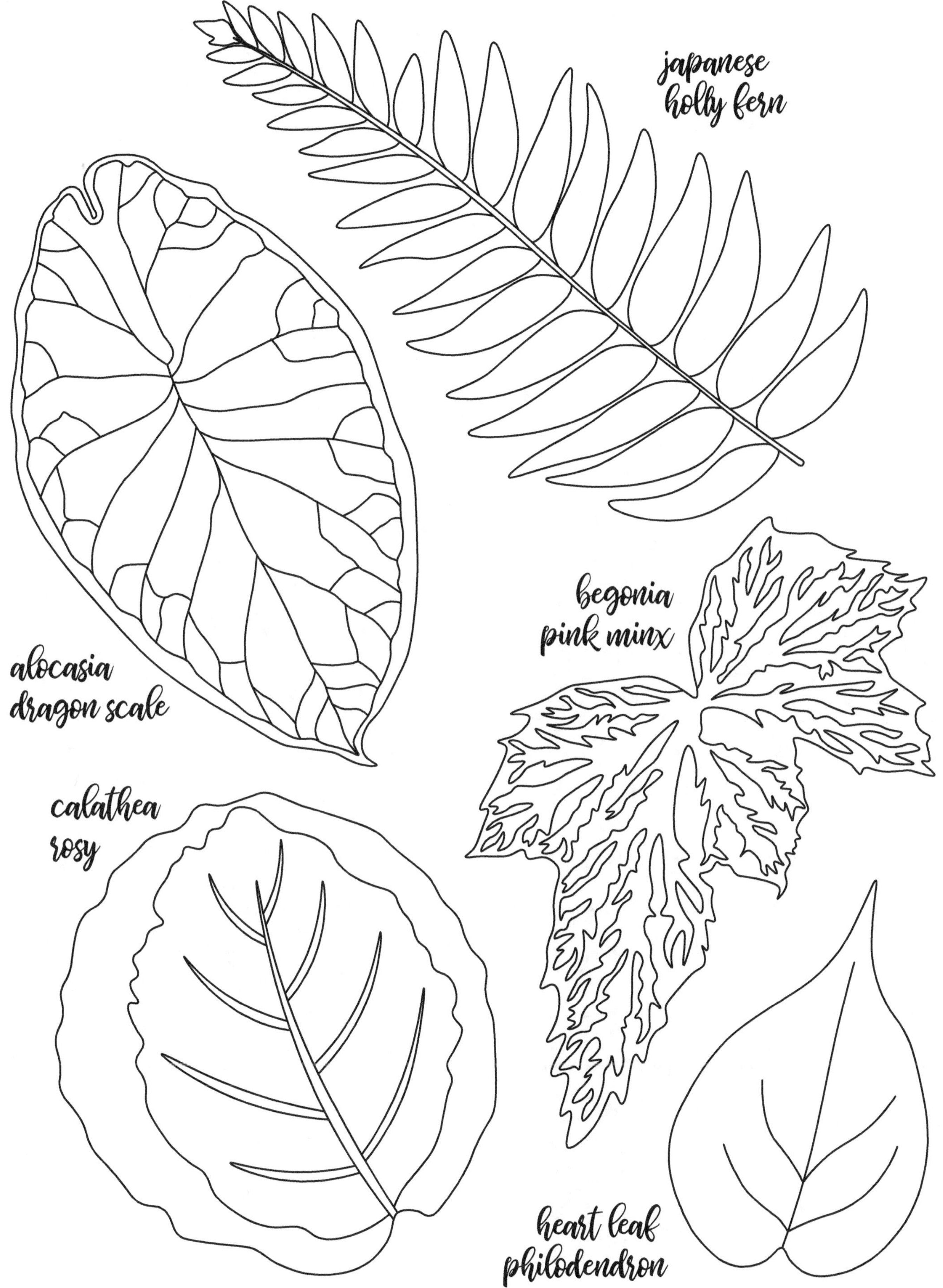

japanese
holly fern
begonia
pink minx
alocasia
dragon scale
calathea
rosy
heart leaf
philodendron

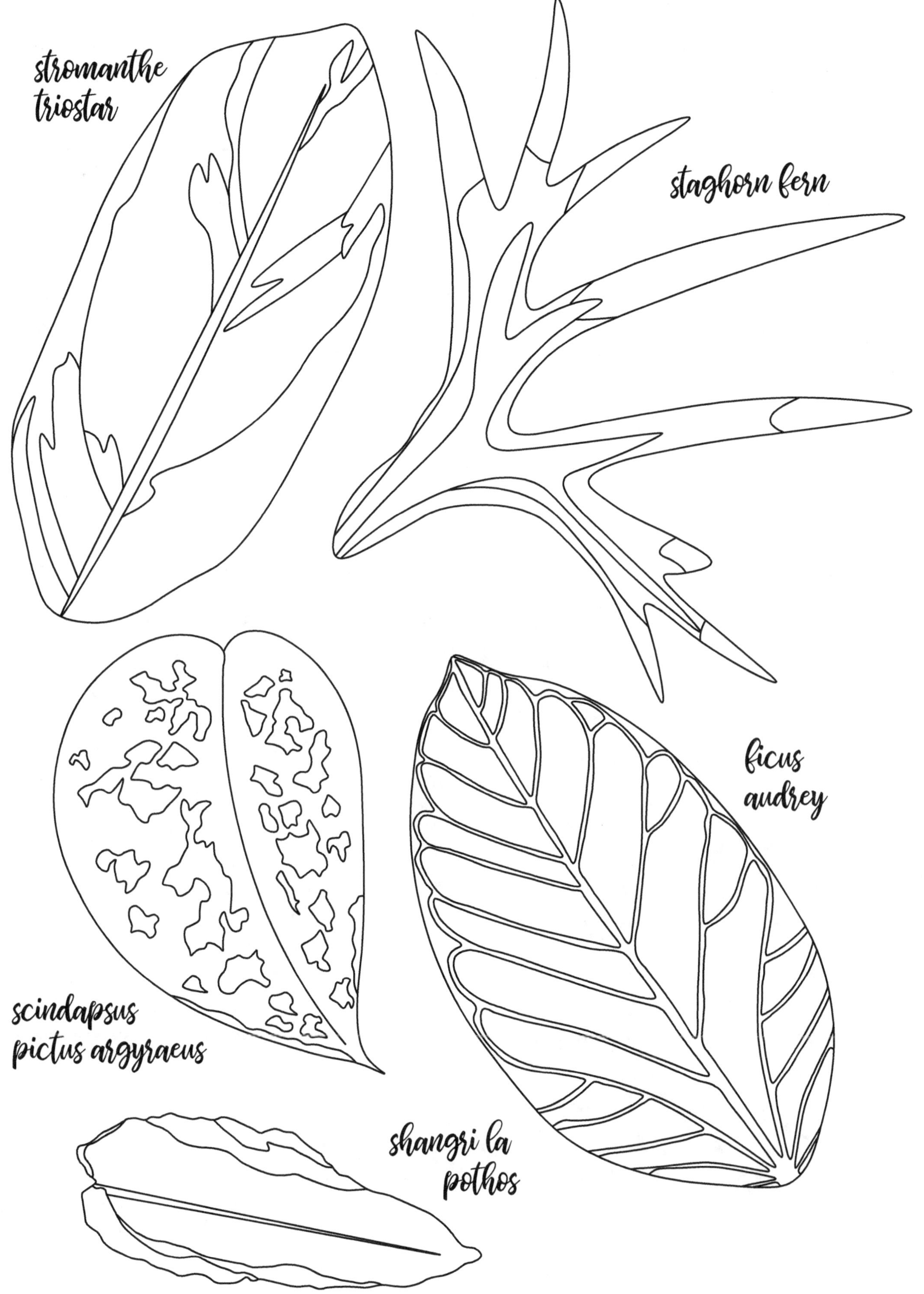

stromanthe
triostar
staghorn fern
ficus
audrey
scindapsus
pictus argyraeus
shangri la
pothos

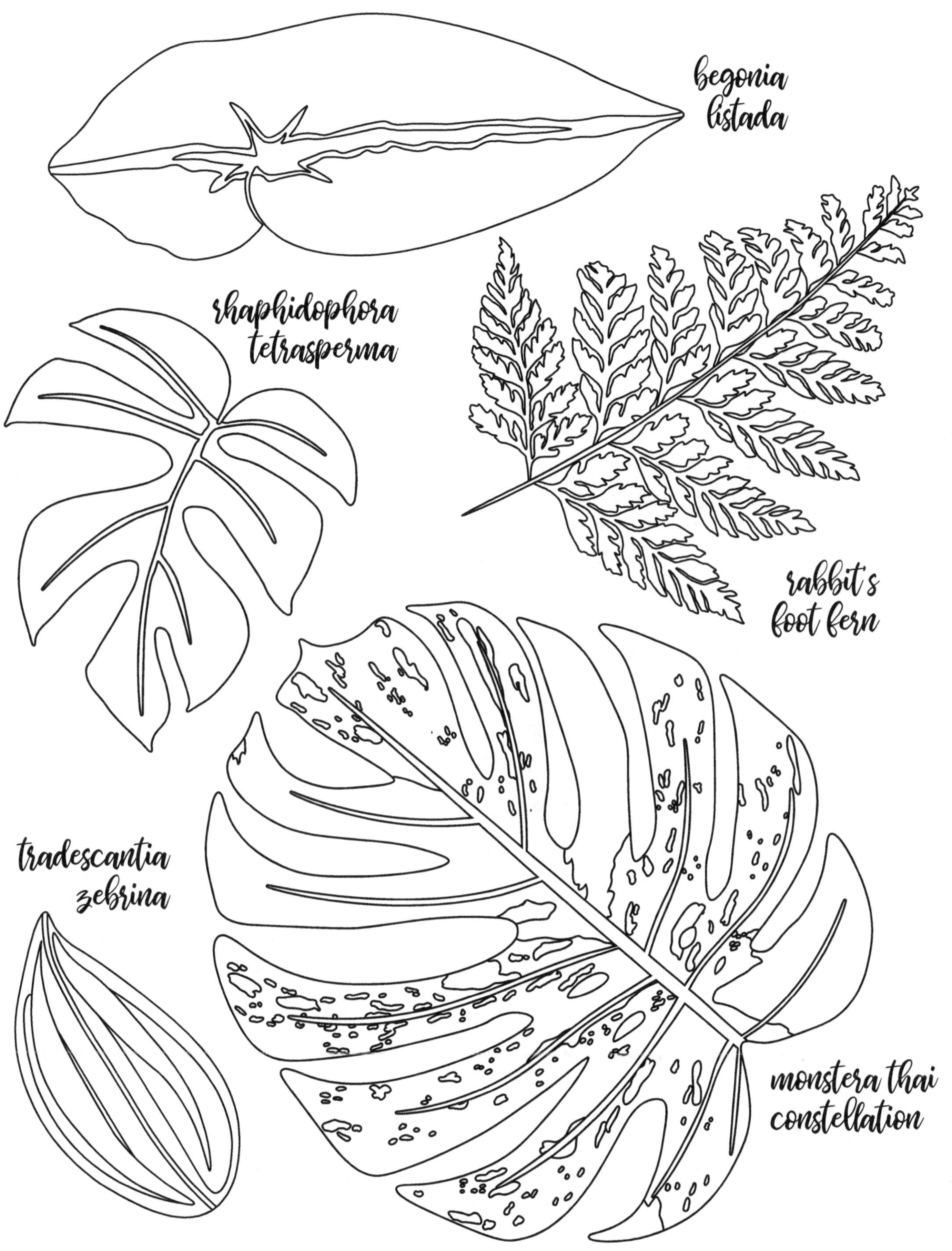

begonia
listada
rhaphidophora
tetrasperma
rabbit's
foot fern
tradescantia
zebrina
monstera thai
constellation

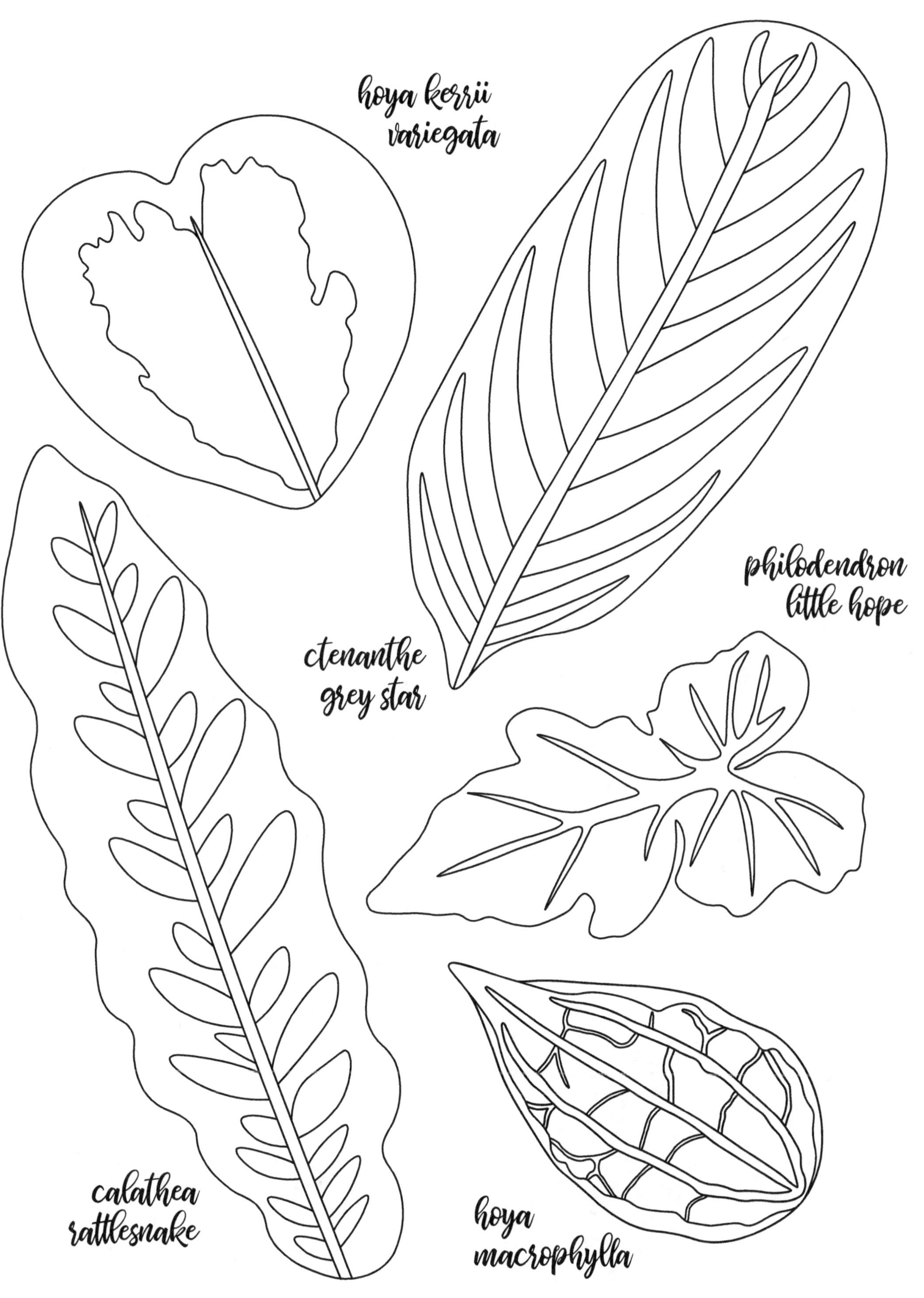

hoya kerrii variegata
philodendron little hope
ctenanthe grey star
calathea rattlesnake
hoya macrophylla

alocasia
stingray
monstera
obliqua
tradescantia
nanouk
philodendron
micans
pothos
n'joy
dracaena
milky way

9 798654 008015